ISBN: 9798850368654

Caroline Seignot

HEY, HUGO, LET'S GO to THE SEASIDE!

Illustrated by

Kim Gregory

Hey, Hugo,

let's go to the seaside

and see what we can find.

Come on Hugo,

Let's go...

LET'S GO!

Hey, Hugo, help me lift up this bucket,

Careful there, and now let's chuck it!

Wow, a SANDCASTLE!

Keep up, and we can explore these rockpools,
come on, Hugo, and bring the tools!

Wow, a CRAB!

Hey, Hugo, let's follow these little prints,

keep up, and look out for some hints.

Wow, a LIGHTHOUSE!

Look right up high, what might we see,

who's that flying over the sea?

Wow, a PUFFIN!

Let's go, Hugo, and search in this cave,

come on, Hugo, you must be brave!

Wow, BATS!

No, Hugo, don't throw it into the sea, you just skim the pebble like me.

Wow, a DOLPHIN!

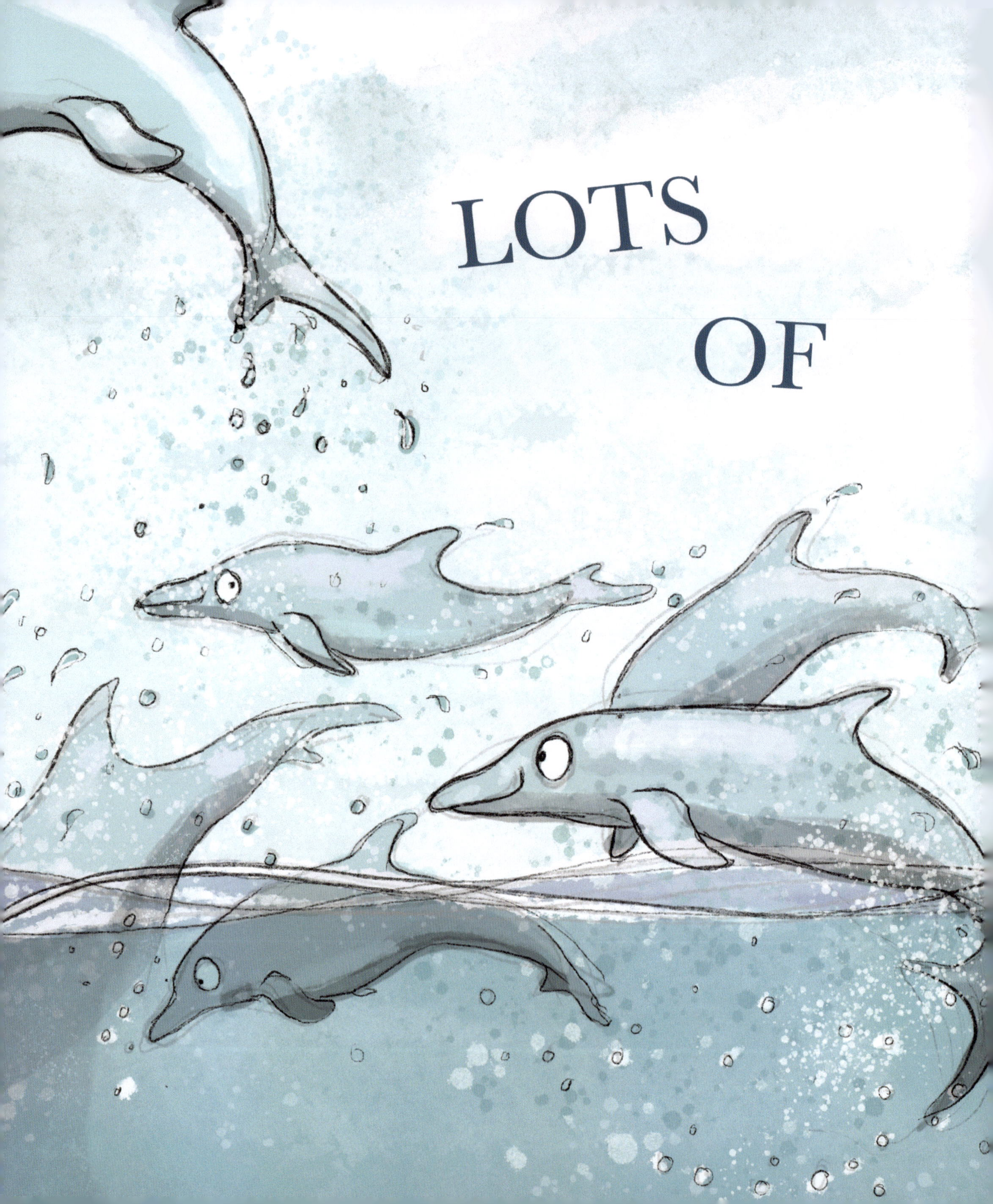

LOTS

OF

DOLPHINS!

Swim slowly here, Hugo, we must take care,

who is that bobbing over there?

Wow, a JELLYFISH!

The horizon is where the sky meets the sea.

Just look, Hugo, who might that be?

Wow, a CORMORANT!

Surf's up, Hugo, now wave and say cheese,

oh no, Hugo, quick, bend your knees!!

Wow, SEAWEED!

Hey, Hugo, come and listen to this seashell,

no, Hugo, no, not THAT shell!

Wow, a HERMIT CRAB!

Hey, let's follow these footprints, Hugo,

I think they are from a BIG GULL!

Wow, it IS a BIG GULL,

and a DONKEY!

HA

BUMP!

Keep going further back there, Hugo,

now look how far I can throw!

Wow, a SHIPWRECK!

A sword, an eye patch, a pirate's hat,

I wonder where we will find the map?

Wow, BARNACLES!

That's it, Hugo, send your kite way up high,

let it go, right up in the sky!

Wow, a CUTTLEFISH!

These seaside adventures side by side,

I know exactly what we will find...

ICE CREAM!

Printed in Great Britain
by Amazon